LE RNING SF

D0718808

A Personal Perspective on the Future of
Social Work and Social-Care Services in the UK

Peter Gilroy OBE

A Personal Perspective on the Future of Social Work and Social-Care Services in the UK

by Peter Gilroy, for Kent Social Services

Peter Gilroy has asserted his right in accordance with the *Copyright, Designs and Patents Act 1988* to be identified as the author of this work.

© Kent Social Services 2004

Produced by Pavilion Publishing (Brighton) Ltd.

ISBN 1-84196-133-7

Edited by: Jo Hathaway
Design and layout: Jigsaw Design (Worthing)
Printed by: Paterson Printing (Tunbridge Wells)

Peter Gilroy OBE
STRATEGIC DIRECTOR • KENT SOCIAL SERVICES

A PERSONAL PERSPECTIVE ON
the future of

social work
&social-care services

in the UK

Kent County Council | Journal of Integrated Care

Pavilion

Contents

A note from the author

This publication relates my personal perspective on the future of social care, based on my understanding of its evolution historically, published documents, my personal experiences, and those of other people I have spoken and worked with.

Social care has come a long way since the enactment of the Poor Laws; the future of eCommerce, self-assessment, purchase cards, assistive technology (telecare) and a myriad other innovations is going to be an exciting ride, if something of a rollercoaster.

From my perspective, the key to unlocking the potential of social care in the future is embracing change and technology and changing cultures – of service users as well as social workers and, indeed, all those involved in social care.

Some people, I am sure, will disagree with the sentiments and comments expressed here; others will not. The aim is to provoke discussion and raise the profile of what is often a poorly-understood service.

We have a lot to be proud of in social care but there is a lot more we can do; we should be leading the debate rather than reacting to it.

Peter Gilroy OBE
August 2004

Forewords

These are turbulent times for social services departments and directors face the future with some ambivalence.

Our instincts tell us that our service users would benefit from better responses from those mainstream services available to all, like Education and the NHS. Their experience, and ours as their advocates, is one of a constant battle for recognition and inclusion.

This is the opportunity of a generation to set social care right.

Peter's personal contribution to the debate about the future of social care is timely and challenging.

Andrew Cozens
President, Association of Directors of Social Services, 2003–04

Let your people go?

You won't agree with everything in Peter Gilroy's publication – I certainly don't – but it was not written with that end in mind. It is a 'personal perspective', but with one extra dimension of validity over my perspective or yours. Here is someone who is prepared to take a lead, stick out his neck, try to get his ideas heard nationally as well as implemented in his Kent backyard. It is worth remembering that this is a Director running the largest social services in the country for many years (three stars) with a reputation for innovation. This publication is an unusual and idiosyncratic response to a challenge laid down originally by the ADSS president.

Since, by picking up this publication, you are likely to be concerned about the future of social services generally or social work as a profession, you should read it through. It would be good if you ended up wanting to take things further yourself, publishing your thoughts and challenges, and maybe by putting extra weight behind a potential movement?

This foreword is my opportunity to say what I think. I was invited to write it by Pavilion Publishing for whom I have been a journal editor for 12 years, combined at times with a job in social-services management and more latterly with work in research and development in integrated care. I began to think 10 years ago that the *Local Authority Social Services Act* needed to be repealed. Most social services departments had by then warmly welcomed the 'vote of confidence' that surprisingly came towards the end of the bleak Thatcher years in the shape of the responsibility for the community care reforms. At the time some wag warned that this was 'a poisoned chalice'. I didn't see it myself at the time, but gradually it began to look right: taking the money in the form of a specific grant ceded power from local government to central government, and this has been ruthlessly reinforced by New Labour's ministers. It also marked the start of greater internal division between adult and children's social services. Cumulatively damaged by the child protection scandals, squeezed to 'deliver' on more specific grants and performance targets, and seen as a way of improving NHS performance, social services capacity to engage creatively with its own communities was drained. People-processing and heavier administration inevitably changed the jobs that workers had to do.

It is a pity that the government can't see its way to putting at least part of the NHS under more direct local-authority influence or control, eg public health; but the government is dead right that the old ways of doing things have to go if the vulnerable people who rely on services are going to get a better deal. The poison from the chalice has been long-lasting. Even if it means more losses and pain, and for the sake of values held dear, take the antidote now!

The reality is that the most vulnerable individual members of our society have needs which cannot be met simply by one professional or agency: the locally-based multi-disciplinary team is the only viable future model, empowered with devolved budgets and trusted professional discretion. For people with less complex needs, a host of responsive innovations are already emerging, eg the so-called single point of access (call centres) which can do a lot rather quickly. The Government is right to want to modernize all this and improve the experiences of patients, carers, and service users. But organisational and professional empires need to be overthrown, and their tasks and responsibilities supported to co-evolve to create better services... there should be no need for take-over, nor threat. Noone knows the best or correct way of doing this; but enthusiasm for learning and working together, shaping new provision in response to the needs and views of local users and carers, would be a good start. This is the antidote.

One thing that all this has meant is that, even after a quarter of a century and more, a key part of Seebohm's vision had not been realized: a strong social-work profession. The paradox I see is that the other part of his vision, a strong voice in local authorities for what he called welfare, and which we might now call social inclusion, has predominated (and needs to continue). However, the bigger social services departments (SSDs) seemed to become within the local authority, the less authority and professional discretion the social workers seemed to have. They are now more bound by procedure and administration than ever: they are functionaries not professionals and, in childcare work, the overwhelming emphasis is on managing the risks associated with the job, less in direct contact with the children. Although specialist areas like adoption or mental health provide a more optimistic picture, in the mainstream the near-monopoly employer has not enhanced their social-work professionalism – which should be a force for good for people needing help. No wonder it is hard to recruit and retain, and impossible to start a discourse other than about the pressures of the job. This has done the reputation of SSDs no good at all, hence the independence of Sure Start and the Children's Fund when they were started (a vote of no confidence), and the search for a new model of provision in last year's green paper on children's services. An even worse symptom of the malaise is that, having now been thrown a professional lifeline by government through the new registration requirements, many social workers are on the verge of spurning it in their apparent demoralization or apathy. Wake up folks! This is the best opportunity you've had in years.

It may take a while to achieve, but the benefit to vulnerable people of high-quality social work will only stand a chance of being realized if we have a wider variety of employers. Primary Care Trusts, GPs and NHS Trusts could all use social workers, and would consider professional social-work staff alongside the allied health professions, and support the development of the specialist skills they need over time. Confident social workers would confront any tendency towards the imposition of the dreaded 'medical model' with empowered service users on their side; and, in any event, government policy and standards are clearly and unambiguously supportive of the holistic person-centred approach. This is an opportunity to be grabbed by social work. The implementation of *Every Child Matters* (DoH, 2003) could also offer similar diversity of employment opportunity, with a resultant need for social workers to take care to establish their own professional identity alongside teachers, psychologists, health visitors and other community workers, and develop their specialisms. Commissioning mechanisms in the local authority could also help to sustain independent-sector employment opportunities, with more professional social work practised in residential, day and community settings – free from the management-dominated career structures of SSDs. It may not need the Act to be repealed, but something should come to symbolize the hope of a better environment for practice, and more direct care.

When you read this book, you will see that Peter Gilroy has laid out all the important themes, and I can find no fault with much of the material and argument he has assembled. You will nevertheless observe that Peter is cagey by saying 'social work at its best', and uses the joined-up phrase 'social work and social care' repeatedly. I guess he would not have done this ten years ago, maybe even five? Why is it that current parlance seems to determine that social care is in fashion, and social work is not? Well done, Peter, for at least letting social work share the sentences… but language tells us things. The nature of care can be easily defined and programmed, so it will never be seen as inherently a profession; it is accepted as something that all of us can do in our private lives, and is an overlay for many working lives, viz 'a caring doctor', 'a teacher who really cares about his pupils'. History has determined that care is the role of 'unqualified' staff in residential, foster, day and domiciliary services, and of enthusiastic amateurs. Unlike professional social work, it is never going to be at the core of the multi-disciplinary team; but without it, the work of doctors, therapists, social workers, and other specialists can come to nought. It is vital, but not valued enough in practice. Last year, nurses took a knock when they were accused of being 'too posh to wash': the same sort of dilemma about care affects that profession too. But it was an unfair slur: the segmentation of roles will always be needed. Most importantly, clarity about accountability is an inherent, but often fudged, consequence.

So where is social care to reside? Is it really a good enough basis for a separately-governed local-authority service? I think not. Universal services like health and education wish to acquire the resource it represents, for perfectly good reasons. Might they ultimately do better by it?

I say let your people go. But, paraphrasing Voltaire, although you may disagree with what I have to say, I trust you will defend to the death my right to say it. This is a critical debate which needs immediate attention, and urgent solutions.

Peter Thistlethwaite
Editor, Journal of Integrated Care

Introduction

In his Presidential Address to the Association of Directors of social services in October 2003, Andrew Cozens called for a new, radical and comprehensive vision for social services that recognises and responds to the aspirations of our services users, and commands confidence in the wider community. Further to this, in his speech on 22 April 2004, Dr Stephen Ladyman, Parliamentary Under-Secretary of State for Health, sought involvement and comment on the future of social care. This paper takes up that challenge and provides a personal perspective.

Writing a personal contribution to the important and ongoing debate upon the future of social work and social care is a very real challenge. The principal themes, dilemmas and issues for consideration identified through such discussions are in themselves weighty and often complex. This paper will seek to identify a range of significant developments to date and, in so doing, provide the context for a commentary upon the key opportunities and challenges for local government, social care and social work. It is important to acknowledge that these terms overlap considerably and as a result are often used interchangeably in such discussions. I have attempted where possible to separate out such themes through the main body of the paper. The conclusions attempt to integrate the emerging themes by providing recommendations for policy makers, and strategic directors, as well as for those directly involved in the delivery of services – be they managers, workers or service users.

The story so far...

The history of social care from initial Poor Laws in 1598 to the Seebohm Report of 1968 and beyond; the early stigmatisation of 'social services' and the beginning of modernisation in the 1990s and early 21st Century, highlights the increasing awareness of the need for social care, and the conflict between welfare and control

The history of social work and social care has to be understood within the context of the wider governance of welfare in the United Kingdom. Perhaps the most significant and enduring point of departure for any such discussion would be the Poor Laws dating back to 1598. The Poor Laws were significantly revised in 1834 due to drivers as diverse as administration difficulties that led to parishes unable to deliver a common standard, the major changes of the Industrial Revolution and associated rapid population-movement and growth. The reforms ensured support for the poor remained lower than that available to the working labourer and made no provision outside of the workhouse. The result was relief against utter destitution delivered within a punitive and stigmatising system that actively deterred people from using it. This may have provided due incentive for individuals to support themselves wherever possible; however, it did little to address the causes of their distress or promote independence and wellbeing.

Despite the growing involvement of many voluntary and charitable organisations (including religious organisations and the development of the hospital almoner), all of which were actively working to alleviate the worst excesses of poverty and disadvantage, there was an increasing acknowledgement throughout the 19th Century of the inadequacy of social provision. International competitiveness and influence, both economically and militarily, were perceived to be a threat if changes were not made to the health and social condition of the population. The turn of the 20th Century saw a formalisation of welfare and social care extended through the passing of the *Old Age Pensions Act* and the *Children's Act 1908*.

The Poor Law doctrines continued to drive legislation and administration of social support until the post-World War II period. This period witnessed significant reforms including the introduction of National Insurance, National Assistance and the National Health Service. It would be impossible to provide any historical account, however brief, and not pay due attention to the influence of the *1968 Seebohm Report* that led to the establishment of social-services departments in 1971. Just as the Poor Laws had done before, notions of the deserving and undeserving poor continued to influence philosophical debate. The implications of the Report and the extent to which its original intentions have been realised to date continue to exercise policy makers and managers alike; in particular, its messages continue to influence attempts to find an effective balance between the different drivers prompting increasingly specialist and generalist workers, teams and organisations. This is further complicated by local differentiation of services, which changes the way in which services, teams and workers are organised and interact with one another nationwide.

The 1990s saw yet more reform, notably through the increasing dominance of care management and the separation of provision and commissioning, as typified by the *1986 Griffiths Report* and the reforms established by the *NHS and Community Care Act 1990*. Social work, and the delivery of social care, became increasingly outcome-focused. Children's services faced the need to be increasingly reflective following the publication in 1995 of *Child Protection Messages from Research*. This document identified the need to begin what is now widely referred to as the 'refocusing debate'. The benevolence and well-intended aims and aspirations of social work were pitted against outcomes that highlighted not only ineffective practice and use of resources, but also the potential for further harm to be caused.

Such challenges endure to this day, as does the widely acknowledged tension that results from social work and social care operating, often simultaneously, within discourses of welfare and control. It is likewise impossible to discount the enduring influence of public inquiries and serious case-reviews following failings in the development of social work and social care. It is the messages for the future of the social-work profession to which this paper now turns.

What is the future for social workers and the social-work profession?

Current themes, initiatives – qualified professionals

Current themes and initiatives emerging in social work, including training and the hybrid/holistic nature of responsibilities and accountabilities for a wide range of workers from a wide range of backgrounds. This section focuses on the development of training and increase in qualifications/professionalism alongside the multi-disciplinary nature of the future both for those practising and those starting out

In this section, the paper sets out the current themes and initiatives that are shaping the roles and responsibilities held by individual social workers, as well as including considerations as to the future direction for the emerging social-work profession. The Institute for Public Policy Research (IPPR) report *From Welfare to Wellbeing* (2002) presents an interesting perspective, a summary of which is given overleaf:

*The world of 2020 could see social work as we
know it dissolved into its constituent functions and
competencies, and redistributed across the map of
new initiatives. Generic social-work practice and
training could fade away, to be replaced by more
specialised and focused developments based around
the newly emerging "social exclusion" professions
and the newly-integrated agencies. Hybrid
occupations will almost certainly emerge,
incorporating elements from several existing
professions.*

*However, against these trends the strength of the
new social-work degree will exert pressure to keep
social work intact. This could be achieved in a
number of ways. The development of specialised
pathways in social work and social care, and of
joint training and education with other professions,
need not be seen as the end of social work but as the
next chapter in an evolving story... The interesting
question is the extent to which social work and
social care will stand their ground in the new
agencies and prove to be of value to them. They
will do this best by serving people well, building on
social-care values and skills, and making a full
contribution to both management and practice
development.*

Hughes (2002) in Kendall & Harker (2002) p.90

A personal perspective on the future of social work & social-care services in the UK

This extract identifies potentially differential outcomes for social-work training and the future of the social-work profession. The increasingly hybrid and holistic nature of the responsibilities and accountabilities held by a wide range of workers and agencies within education, health and social care provides fertile ground for extending the influence of social-work theories and approaches. However, if one is to successfully promote long-term solutions to the recruitment- and retention-difficulties facing social work, the social-care industry needs to make significant contribution in the drive to improve vocational opportunities for young people. This could be achieved, in part, by offering in partnership with Education and the colleges, vocational placements for young people aged 14 and above. Social-work education and training itself has always drawn upon a wide range of academic disciplines, integrating these to varying success into training and preparation for would-be social-work practitioners. This year sees social work becoming a 'protected title' and, as referred to above, the first students commence compulsory degree-level training. The ongoing consolidation of social-work training should be underpinned with generic modules with regard to theory, research, policy and practice that will need to be eclectic in approach.

Specialisation can then be developed as part of the competence framework in post-graduate development. An allied development is that of extending multi-disciplinary modules for all

**professional disciplines in education, health
and social care. Such developments could be
encouraged with multi-agency student resource-
centres that would handle co-ordination and
some placement responsibilities. This would
provide a framework of competence whilst
retaining the necessary focus and disciplines
within each professional grouping.**

The role of universities

*Looking at the role of universities and organisations in
establishing effective research mechanisms and extending
the evidence-base underpinning social-work practice and
policy*

It would also be a useful step-change to have a closer
interchange between those who teach and those in
the public sector who manage services. We can learn
something here in the way in which industry is now
moving closer to the universities, colleges and schools
and the vocational debate critical to the continued
economic improvement within the UK. I think a creative
inter-change of talent and the placement of lecturers as
part of their own development into working organisations
would be helpful. It will be necessary to ensure that
organisations and universities establish effective
mechanisms for promoting high-quality critical
social-work research. As social-work employers become
increasingly enmeshed with providers of training,

research and evaluation, there is a real opportunity to extend the evidence-base necessary to underpin effective social-work practice and social policy. This will require social-work employers to be increasingly reflective and self-questioning to enable difficult questions to be asked, to respond to challenging messages and integrate such developments within the development of policy and practice. Such developments will provide an opportunity for social work to learn more by evaluating and disseminating 'what works' as opposed to the present overwhelming dominance of resources and attention afforded to failings, whether individual or systematic.

Outcomes and ethics

The importance of individualised and customised products leading to better outcomes, following in the steps of commercial companies; the role of positive outcomes from influences to behaviour eg personal relationships, networking and therapies

The increasing importance of the code of ethics and competence framework leading to a strong, shared value-base put into practice that values diversity, advocacy and promotes independence

Research suggests that where producers and consumers collaborate to produce more personal and customised products, better outcomes are achieved both for individuals and for society as a whole (Kendall, 2001). This is something that commercial enterprises have long identified as central to success in the marketplace, investing considerable resources in such endeavours. Of course, it would be possible here to embark upon a lengthy discussion as to how outcomes are defined and by whom. After all, social work is often engaged with those who find their voices especially hard to hear and their experiences almost impossible to have accepted, verified and responded to.

Research is interesting in looking at positive outcomes of change in terms of influences to behaviour. A number of pieces of social-work research internationally have found that in terms of effecting change, the following are very significant:

1. **Personal relationships:** this is interesting because we all live our lives through relationships and, regardless of the level, it is hardly possible if staff-turnover rates are such that the public never see the same person twice. Outcomes are 40% more effective for those service users who regularly see the same social-care worker;

2. **Networking:** the ability to look across communities outside of one's specialism and behave accordingly in accessing appropriate information of service to the user. In terms of its impact on successful outcomes, this represents 45% importance;

3. Therapies: it is interesting that the application of different forms of therapies for individuals and families does not represent the same impact although significant for some. Outcomes are 15% more likely to be successful for service users who have experienced therapy.

Lambert (1992), Miller *et al.* (1997) and Assay & Lambert (1999) in McKeown (2000)

The code of ethics, as recently issued by the General Social Care Council, has also been revised, no longer including specific references to anti-oppressive practice. Additionally, social workers will increasingly be operating within clear 'competency-based' frameworks that will necessitate organisations to consider how they can continue to enable innovative and creative social-work practice within increasingly established roles, responsibilities and accountabilities that direct the tasks and duties of social workers.

The vision here is for highly-competent social-work professionals, who are able to work in a variety of settings, in partnership with users and carers, which will necessitate a strong shared value-base and have the skills to put those values into practice. The values are those that are intrinsic to social work at its best:

- empowering individuals and communities;
- promoting independence;
- taking an holistic and person-centred approach;
- valuing difference and diversity and determined advocacy etc.

However, there is a danger that, notwithstanding these aspirations, professional cultures can disempower and diminish the potential of users and communities to sustain and decide for themselves the shape of services they require. It is therefore important for social work and care to advocate social models of disability and continue to break away from paternalistic cultures.

The long-term view for social workers

Long-term future for social workers – perhaps fewer but better trained and better paid as part of a family of social care and other professions

The long-term view would suggest that there will be fewer fieldwork social-workers; where they do exist, they will be better paid and better trained. Social workers will need to be as able to contribute to social-policy development as to employing interpersonal skills effectively with service users. Social workers will therefore be highly competent working in a range of settings and a number of virtual teams in any given week. The USA provides an interesting perspective on how one can ensure that social work retains a unique contribution in assisting with the broad outcome of improving life-chances for children by promoting family stability and children's emotional, personal and social development (Blank, 2003).

This is likely to renew tensions with regard to the range of roles and responsibilities held by social workers, as opposed to other education, health and social-care staff; whether some of the existing social-work tasks disappear or are undertaken by allied health and social-care workers remains to be seen.

It is worth reminding ourselves that for every qualified social worker, there are approximately 30 social-care workers in different settings and agencies who provide most of the hands-on care in the social-care industry. The debate about nursing and the impact of increasing professionalism on the way tasks are carried out on the wards may provide an indicator as to the future debate for social work. It may be helpful to consider what is already known about the implications of implementing varying models of care-management in identifying such dilemmas.

The task of balancing effective intervention and provision of services with the drive for competent care-management built upon the foundation of 'holistic' assessments could lead to more confusion; despite each client having one named social worker, they could find themselves being offered support by a variety of different individuals.

The opportunities for developing a family of (hands-on) social-care professionals will be significant as we move into the next five to ten years. The innovations within the health and social-care economy in the UK in this area need to be celebrated and strategically brought into the mainstream as soon as possible. It is to this wider remit of social care that this paper now turns.

The development of social-care services

Adapting to radical change

The constant need for social care to adapt and develop in line with radical changes already underway to meet future needs; holistic, preventative services requiring a cultural shift from 'caring' to 'promoting independence'; shift in public attitudes and expectations – demands for a more customer-focused approach and advocating 'social models'

As referred to above, the IPPR report *From Welfare to Wellbeing* provides a similarly elegant summary of the future vision for social care:

> *Our vision for social care in 2020 is that it will seek to promote wellbeing by empowering individuals and their communities. The sector will provide high quality, outcome-oriented services that are universally used by those who need them, while also being universally supported by those who do not. The predominant focus will be on delivering holistic, preventive services for vulnerable groups with highly specialised and targeted interventions for those in need.*

Kendall & Harker (2002) p.20

This extract highlights many themes for discussion and the need for considerable development if such aims and aspirations are to be fully realised.

It is hard to point to a period in the recent past when the provision of social care and support has not been subject to critique, reform and re-evaluation. As identified in the introduction, the development of social care to date has not been linear. However, the need to adapt and change has been a constant. This should not, however, come as a surprise nor should this be seen as a sign of continued failure. The context within which social care is delivered is likewise subject to ongoing change thereby impacting upon expectations in an active process. This results in the need for constant readjustments for workers, teams and organisations.

It is not unreasonable to suggest that social care has been (and will continue to be) complementary to the overriding strategic objectives set within current government policy. In part this is due to the continued evolution and re-labelling of social care that presently places its 'raison d'être' and value base within the context of promoting independence. Much has recently been stated about the apparently insurmountable resistance to change within the public sector. I propose, however, that radical change to the means of delivering on such objectives is already taking place and will continue to mould the work and organisation of social care in the future. It is possible to point to an ongoing culture shift between 'caring for people' and 'promoting independence' across social care. The roots of current programmes and initiatives, however, are rarely truly innovative in their conception. It is possible to see echoes within the approaches such as Harold Wilson's 'hand up not hand out' or indeed in the essays of Adam Smith (1976). Professional practitioners, whatever their label, find themselves grappling intellectually and practically with changing behaviour and provision within this framework. It is necessary therefore to identify connections and continuity, whilst highlighting the changes that this demands of staff and organisations alike.

The differences today concern a fundamental shift in public attitudes which demands a customer-care approach on the part of public services. Therefore, central to achieving such a cultural shift is the need to continue to advocate 'social models' and an understanding and approach that is characterised not upon dependent, paternalistic relationships of intervention, but rather one that is characterized by partnerships that are increasingly led and owned by service users and carers. This will not only consolidate developments to date but will also potentially greatly strengthen social care. This will not be without its obstacles, however, and if it is to be successful it has to bridge the differences in power and status that may prevent medical professions following similar paths.

As already stated, arguably the most significant driver for change is growing public expectation and a widening of the means through which it is articulated and presented. It is impossible therefore to adequately address the future of social care, without considering the perspective of service users, carers and the communities in which they live.

Choice – social-care tourism?

Choice is a key feature of the future. It is possible as mobility increases that people will seek social care in warmer EU countries. Getting the simple things right matters and we need to be obsessional about this in terms of customer care

The language and discourse of 'choice' presently dominate the political arena for the future of public services. Social-care services will undoubtedly form an important part of such debate. It is also important to note that such choice will not be limited to local or even national considerations. Increasing mobility may result in service users seeking particular care services in warmer EU countries. Delivery of social-care services themselves is likely to become increasingly international. Although there is much public scepticism about the reality of 'choice' for consumers of public services, it is clear that success of social-care services will increasingly be measured by perceptions of relevance, responsiveness and sensitivity of provision. Public services must become obsessional in the process of modernising around the simple issues of customer care. Getting the simple things right first time is a critical success factor in altering public perception.

The role of technology in establishing independence

Role of technology in increasing choice and responsiveness eg web-based technology, self-assessment, purchase cards and telecare[1] or telehealth[2]. Technology as a means to an end. Enabling communities and individuals to look after themselves and build on the support of friends and families who already provide the majority of care

Service users and their carers are increasingly likely to direct the future of social care through web-enabled self-assessments, self-managed packages of care and direct payments, as facilitated by policy changes such as the *Health and Social Care Act 2001*. Such developments are likely to continue as technology improves. Further examples – such as the purchase cards enabling 'real time purchasing', fast-track development of

---

1 **Telecare:** 'The remote or enhanced delivery of health and social-care services to people in their own home by means of telecommunications and computer-based systems' (Barnes *et al*, 1998, p169)

2 **Telehealth** is broadly described as the use of electronic information and communication technologies to provide and support health care when distance separates the participants. It involves the use of modern two-way interactive audio/video telecommunications, computers and telemetry, in order to deliver health services to remote patients and to facilitate information exchange between primary care physicians and specialists at some distance from each other. (Explanation from General Practice Computing Group website.)

telecare and telehealth (the latter offering real radicalisation in the way people manage chronic ill health) – offer a fundamental change in the way the health economy and social-care work in partnership to self-manage care. This would be particularly true, when developed alongside imaginative innovations in housing (Smart design). This would enable service users and carers to maintain their independence wherever possible and change the way they engage with health and social-care services. Technology, however, must always be a means to an end. Nevertheless, it does have the potential to alter fundamentally the way in which much of the public-sector services are delivered and provides a real power base for users and carers to shape the services they want. It will need to be balanced against ensuring competent professionals offering, where appropriate, fast-track face-to-face assessment and hands-on services. Therefore, social-care services must explore how to ensure provision of bespoke holistic services for individuals with even the most complex needs. Alongside this, however, there is also a need to recognise that reliance solely upon individual outcomes are likely to be less effective and efficient than collective and inclusive services. There is a central role for social-care services in building community-capacity and self-determination in the broadest sense. This will require revolutionizing the means in which information and support is provided, enabling individuals and communities to look after themselves. After all, friends and families already provide the majority of care and support and will continue to do so. The growth of a highly-personalised and devolved framework for social care is evidenced in the range of 'needs led' and 'holistic' assessments which have already seen social care transformed for the better. However, more and more, these are undertaken within discourses for service delivery that are increasingly rights-based. The tensions and dilemmas facing social care (and health care for that matter) as it seeks to respond to needs and rights of service users and carers within the constraints of public financial resources will continue. These are especially evident when addressing the critical issues of protecting individuals and the wider public. Social-care services are continuing to refine their responses, following the implications of the *Human Rights Act 1998*.

A difficult balance – eligibility and access

Vicious circle of targeting specialised services and resources whilst at the same time widening access and prevention – balancing immediate response (often costly) and longer-term preventative activity. Some benefits already being reaped in this area

Social-care services have increasingly been characterised by the formulation of eligibility criteria, screening and other mechanisms for gate-keeping whilst at the same time actively trying to widen access. There are considerable pressures for social-care services in how to provide preventative services, develop community infrastructure and promote ongoing developments in education and childcare, whilst also targeting specialist services and resources. Eligibility criteria may result in the refusal of support and assistance that is characterised by being limited, both in respect of the range of objectives it addresses and the time taken to achieve results. Such action is likely to result in more extensive and longer-term provision in later life as people become more dependent; this will directly impact upon the provision of preventative services, hence keeping such barriers to service high.

For many years social-care services have been stuck in this vicious cycle of having to invest heavily in responding to immediate needs within the contexts of child protection, looked-after children and residential care. This has often been at the expense of longer-term preventative activity. Recent years, however, have seen considerable resources put into the local education, health and social-care economy and we are just beginning to reap the benefits. The task ahead will be to develop innovative approaches to evidence the long-term savings and benefits enabled through such investment.

Developments in local government and social policy

Accountability – the national and local context

Context of governance and accountability both nationally and locally along with the impact of international issues eg security and migration. The increasing prevalence of performance indicators, leagues tables and the impact of a plethora of regulation and bureaucracy leading to issues of confidence and morale. Instead we should focus on more select central policy-objectives that would then increase local accountability and reduce overheads

It is impossible to deliver any coherent vision of the future for social work and social care without acknowledging the context of governance and accountability both nationally and locally within which they operate. Additionally, the effects of globalisation and international issues such as migration, security and citizenship are increasingly impacting upon the aspirations and policies of local government.

The present Government has already instituted many reforms as part of the 'modernising' agenda. This has been characterised by the increasing prevalence of performance indicators, league tables, scrutiny of management action-plans through a plethora of bureaucracy and quasi monitors and regulators. The outcomes have been mixed but a general sense has emerged, even for those authorities perceived as top-performing, that the benefits of freedoms and flexibilities have not matched the heavy weight of bureaucracy relating to the demands for information by central government. It is also time to reflect on the impact of health and safety legislation on the social-care industry. The population seems to have been encouraged to be more litigious and risk averse; this is now impacting upon costs and our ability to innovate. It is time to review the legislation and bring back a degree of common sense and balance. If we do not, we will be subsuming millions of pounds of public money on unnecessary civil actions. American experience is a salutory example of what is ahead of us if we do not redress the balance.

The negative aspects of the present regime of central government promoting change through regulation and naming-and-shaming failing authorities is likely to produce diminishing returns. Over-regulation can perversely diminish confidence and create a culture of indecision and low morale. In their place should be an increasing focus upon a limited number of outcomes related to central policy-objectives. With some caveats, Public Service Agreements and the development of Public Service Boards potentially provide an opportunity to move forward and create a new relationship with central government. This will reduce overhead costs and increase local accountability to provide high-quality services and customer care. It would also enable public services to direct their energies towards 'front-end competencies' and deliver continuity and synergy of services within a highly-devolved management culture.

This will fit with developments in inspection already being seen within OFSTED and the years of experience within what was the Social Services Inspectorate, the latter in the forefront of talking to users and carers when evaluating social services.

The importance of the ability to self-assess, regulate and implement change, as well as measuring performance is now being acknowledged. In a similar way for that identified for social work and social care, local government will have the opportunity to begin to evidence and learn from best practice, effective services and good outcomes rather than failings and deficiencies.

eCommerce provides the means by which such lessons and developments can be disseminated, hence engendering more confidence in local government and thereby curtailing the tendency for centralisation.

A positive approach to motivation

Continual demands for structural change and reorganisation are counter-productive and lead to poor motivation, increased costs and rarely an improvement in outcomes. They should instead focus on customers, stability and competence and a new way of managing change that puts the emphasis on integrating processes to avoid new multi-agency silos

Continued demands for structural change and reorganisation as a mechanism for delivering real improvements for individuals, community and public protection may prove counterproductive in the medium term. The consequences may well be a loss of intellectual competence and focus, low morale and a poorly-motivated workforce. Historically, transactional overhead costs increase, but productivity and quality may not necessarily improve. I must admit to being surprised at how many able people are surprised by this outcome.

The systems within the mixed economy of social care will always be complex and it would be much better for them to concentrate on:

1. The customer;
2. Stability and competence at the front-end of the service;
3. A new way of managing change.

In my view, this brings an optimism about managing the challenge and empowers frontline services to be creative and innovative in the services offered (through multi-agency arrangements) to users and their carers. The route to better outcomes for individuals with health and social-care needs is through integrated care-pathways organised around evidence-based protocols which specify the roles, responsibilities and sequence of interventions by the different professionals involved. In other words, integrating processes (eg, single assessments) and building services around the user (multi-agency packages) are more likely to achieve good outcomes than setting up functional bureaucracies, eg new children's services. We do not live our lives like this and the tendency to functionalise our culture may ultimately and ironically disempower the public through fragmentation of professional services to the public, with numbers of professionals visiting the same household because of their functional interest. Public protection will also not be served by this process.

The organisational changes that move to functional structures and new multi-disciplinary silos will bring new and quite difficult challenges both in terms of cost-effectiveness and organisational and professional development.

Delivering the vision

Key role of local government in delivering the vision – instrumental in the range of services that local government are accountable for

Local government has a key role in delivering the vision of a society that values difference and diversity, where discrimination on the grounds of race, disability, gender and sexuality is no longer acceptable. Local government can be instrumental in shaping crucial factors such as the style and design of housing, amenities and communities, that can make a direct and creative improvement to quality of life.

There has been a growing obsession with organisational structures and demands for ever-increasing resources to deliver upon continually-expanding mandates. Finding consensus regarding the level of funding for public services is one that always seems to escape agreement by all parties. However, it is possible to find more common ground when focusing upon how existing resources are utilised. In particular one can point to a growing acknowledgement that directing professional services solely upon the problems of today rather than reshaping the business for tomorrow's challenges is destined to fail in the long-term.

An ageing population – future challenges

Impact of demographic changes have been much talked about but an ageing population does not necessarily mean increased demand as health, leisure and employment attitudes change. The biggest challenge is likely to be dementia, in all forms

It is possible to look at the demographics and envisage somewhat of a crisis for the delivery and funding of services in future. In particular such discussions focus upon an ageing population with rightful expectations of a higher quality of life and who are less likely to be as deferential as many whose lives were shaped by economic depression and rationing. Many people eligible for services and assistance presently do not receive them either because those currently available do not fit their needs or perhaps because of the perceived stigma attached to social services.

It should not be assumed, however, that demographic pressures will not be moderated by other factors as they apply to demands upon the health and social-care industries. Attitudes regarding work and leisure are changing. People are staying in employment longer and notwithstanding the current debate about pension funding, most will have greater purchasing power and political influence. It will be in the twilight years, however, where the prevalence of conditions such as dementia will continue to present the greatest challenge to the health and social-care economy.

Local government will itself face having to respond to public opinion as well as providing leadership in shaping expectation. The way in which communities define themselves and their aspirations should be central to local-government strategy. In recent MORI polls factors contributing to safety and independence figure highly. I suggest that in the future people will want social-care services, as they will also obtain the power and choice to purchase what they need. Direct-payment schemes, enabled by developments such as purchase cards and the empowering of service users and carers, will bring new opportunities and challenges with more articulate service users seeking out more flexible and innovative services.

Dynamic and diverse – supporting independence and relationships

Revolutionising how information and services are provided to increase empowerment and move towards 'wellbeing' legislation and away from 'Poor Law' style regimes. A more focused and dynamic contribution that can bring together diverse services

This will require revolutionising the means by which information and support is provided to enable individuals and communities to look after themselves – after all, friends and families continue to provide the majority of care and support. The fostering and development of individual and community responsibility must be integral to any such approach. The provision of information about how to facilitate independence, sustain health and maintain wellbeing, including access to high-quality leisure, learning and social activities will redirect resources from traditional social care.

Moving towards 'wellbeing legislation' from regimes that still display elements of 'poor law' style regimes is essential but not without its difficulties. As mentioned in earlier sections, this represents a significant challenge in redefining the relationship between central and local government. Such relationships are likely to continue to be conflicted unless the competing demands for local government to deliver wellbeing through promoting independence, whilst also managing increasing duties and responsibilities that rest more in the realms of control and surveillance are carefully balanced.

Adopting a clear customer-care focus as part of a public-planning structure built upon a wide-angled view of 'community' will assist local government in retaining and strengthening its position within the health, education and social-care economies, particularly in building community capacity and self-determination in the broadest sense. This, of course, includes housing, employment and the health of the local and national economies. This will require local government to offer a more dynamic contribution as seen from a whole-systems perspective, thematically bringing together a range of diverse, specialist services, to undertake meaningful benchmarking and develop systems enabling them to learn more effectively from each other. These developments are taken up more fully within the final section of this paper.

Conclusions and recommendations

Developing modern public services

Reaffirming the contribution of social work and social care to developing modern public services in the 21st Century. The role of eCommerce and technology

This paper has attempted to reaffirm the contribution of social work and social care within the context of local government to developing a modern public service for the 21st Century. The shifting sands of public attitudes and education suggest that the future is increasingly going to be in responding to the diverse and fluid issues associated with quality of life. Information technology and eCommerce will continue to shape the access to, as well as content and style of public services. I have endeavoured to propose some recommendations that emerge from the themes discussed through the main body of the paper. Although not explicitly presented in such a format, there are messages here for policy makers and strategic planners, as well as those directly involved in the delivery and receipt of services.

National frameworks, local management

Central government is not the best place to determine local activity and detailed targets, but the rationalisation of regulatory schemes and frameworks is welcome along with the role of the new Commission for Social Care Inspection

There has never been a convincing argument that central government is the right place to determine local activities and detailed targets. As noted above, this creates an industry of bureaucracy, quangos and regulators duplicating in some areas and missing others completely. The transactional costs are extremely high and the bureaucracy increasingly complex. I welcome the rationalisation that is taking place nationally in such regulatory schemes and frameworks, especially in moving away from micro-managing performance indicators. I am delighted to say that I have great confidence in the current leadership of the Commission for Social Care Inspection (CSCI) in taking on such challenges and providing a beacon for others in the industry.

Promoting excellence and wellbeing through local government

Development and role of regional teaching clusters in local government and further development of Area and Public Service Agreements and the need for local government to reclaim the role of promoting wellbeing

The development of clusters, possibly on a regional basis, of teaching local authorities, could bolster the ongoing development of local-government excellence and build upon schemes such as 'beacon' authority status and the award of 'three stars'. The example of teaching hospitals or other centres of excellence would provide a useful example of how other systems such as the health economy has developed such resources to help all involved on performance issues.

The development of Public Service Agreements based upon mutuality between central and local government appears to be proving very successful in ensuring organisations focus upon shared goals from the strategic to local level. Public Service Boards, which are currently being piloted, may also help this path. Such programmes have the potential to fundamentally shape the way in which public services change and deliver upon democratic intentions. With the complex relationships within the education, health and social-care economies, further development of such frameworks needs to continue if organisations can be made to be truly accountable for producing positive outcomes when these are dependent upon such diverse influences. Local government should maximise its experience in commissioning, leading, and – at times, not simply managing scrutiny of health but – managing services directly on behalf of the health economy.

Local government should remain the home for the majority of social care and thereby take the lead in the modernisation of public services including drivers that lead to improvements in public health. Amending the *Local Government Act 2000* could be undertaken to increase the 'wellbeing' powers for local government. New forms of organisation that are highly devolved and keep track with developments in eCommerce will be essential if organisations are to be enduring and successful.

Social care and the remit of local government needs to be reclaimed to promote the wellbeing of the whole community as intended by the *Seebohm Report* (1968). This could be initiated by establishing a consensus upon what constitutes positive outcomes and how to work together to make such aims and aspirations a reality for service users, carers and the wider community.

A radical review and the repeal of the remaining inappropriate poor law legislation would also be an important step and would be a very visible move towards the goals of modernisation and promoting independence.

24/7 – looking after customers, supporting staff

Importance of 'People's Centres' and a 24/7 integrated culture, the commercial sector, customer care and importantly, staff care and retention in an increasingly flexible workforce

Portrayal to the public of social services – good news rarely told but we need to be proud of what we have achieved

Services may evolve into 'People's Centres' providing integrated services within the community, both physically and virtually, potentially forming a hub-and-spoke network of general and specialist resources, hence maximizing accessibility. Providing clarity through information available on a 24/7 basis will be the key to the success of such developments. This could include providing information/access points possibly co-locating some services within parts of the commercial-service sector such as supermarkets.

Social-care services and organisations will need to adopt a very clear and robust 'customer care' ethos that ensures consistently high-quality services that are able to respond to the attitudes and judgements made by the public. The customer and perception of need therefore needs to be given a central place in developing services that are competent in balancing stability with

the need to incrementally refocus and reform in light
of many changes.

Social-care employers must consider radical staff
care-and-retention policies, as highly skilled and
motivated staff are successful in delivering upon any
of the objectives outlined here. This will require a
real investment in ongoing professional training and
associated activities to a figure in excess of 2% gross
spend. Staff are likely to be deployed in an increasing
variety of settings and environments through a wide
range of agencies, working ever more in partnership
with service users. To deliver real success, staff will need
to be enabled to operate and stay within communities.
They should then be able to build meaningful partnerships and establish lasting relationships built upon trust.
This will be further assisted by devolved organisations
enabling decisions to be made as close to the ground as
possible. This will necessitate pooling of responsibility
and resources including budgets into multi-agency
contexts.

The route for better outcomes for individuals with
even the most complex needs is through integrated
assessments and pathways. These will need to be built
upon evidence-based protocols specifying the roles,
responsibilities and sequencing of interventions by
the various professionals and other parties involved.
This requires integrating processes, such as single
assessment frameworks, that result in the organisation
and delivery of services around the user by way of

multi-agency packages. It is important that health and social-care services cease to be dominated by functionalist responses and fragmented services. This leads to many professionals visiting the same household with little connection and co-ordination with sometimes dire results for the protection of individuals and the community.

Social work needs to re-define itself as integral to the solution rather than part of the problem. Little is presently heard of the successes of individual workers, teams and agencies in protecting individuals and communities. Likewise, the provision of preventative services rarely hit the headlines in diverting resources or risk away from heavy-end involvement such as child protection, youth offending or, indeed, residential care. Social work has to learn the art of self-promotion to share success and to build upon further advances following improved training and proper accreditation.

Social work will need to find a careful balance between firmly establishing itself as a competent profession, while retaining a clear focus upon the overriding importance of doing the simple things consistently well that is increasingly identified as essential to ensuring positive outcomes. Social work needs to retain, not distil, its sense of self through its value base, and diligently promote social models of understanding throughout society. These core values and associated professional standards will enable the provision of consistently high-quality services and support that are flexible and responsive, driven by users, carers and communities.

Services of the future must have at their core a 'customer-care' ethos and shift away from paternalistic cultures. Attitudes are changing and judgements made by the general public on the quality of public, social-care services will not be determined by what we say but by what they taste, see and feel. They will be the ultimate arbiters as to whether we are serious about modernising public services.

Social work and social services have a lot to be proud of and that should never be underestimated, but there is a lot more to be done and we should be leading this debate rather than reacting to it.

A personal perspective on the future of social work & social-care services in the UK

References

Barnes *et al* (1998) Lifestyle monitoring – technology for supported independence. *Control Engineering Journal*, August 169–174.

Blank M. J. (2003) *Making The Difference: Research and Practice in Community Schools*. Washington, USA: Coalition for Community Schools.

Department of Health (1995) *Child Protection Messages From Research*. CI (95) 22. London: DoH.

Kendal L. (2001) *The Future Patient*. London: IPPR.

Kendal L. & Harker L. (2002) *From Welfare to Wellbeing: The Future of Social Care*. London: IPPR.

Kent County Council (2001) *The Kent Agreement. The Local Public Service Agreement for Kent 2001 to 2004*. Kent: KCC.

McKeown K. (2000) *Supporting Families – A Guide to What Works in Family Support Services for Vulnerable Families*. Dublin: The Department of Health and Children (Stationery Office).

Presidential Address by Andrew Cozens to Association of Directors of Social Services, October 2003.

Seebohm Report (1968) *Report of the Committee on Local Authority and Allied Personal Services*. Cmnd 3703. London: HMSO.

Skinner K. (Ed) (2004) *Community Leadership and Public Health: The role of local authorities*. Kent: The Smith Institute with Kent County Council.

Skinner A. S. & Wilson T. (Eds) (1976) *Essays on Adam Smith*. Oxford: OUP.

Smith A. (unknown) *Essays on Philosophical Subjects*. In: Wightman W. P. D. (Aug '82) *Liberty Classics* 31.

Speech by Stephen Ladyman MP, Parliamentary Under Secretary of State for Community, 19 May 2004: Community Care Live and 22 April 2004 The Association of Social Services Directors Spring Seminar.

Wistow G., Herbert G., Townsend J., Ryan J., Wright D. & Ferguson B. (2002) *Rehabilitation Pathways for Older People after Fractured Neck of Femur: Executive Summary*. Leeds: Nuffield Institute for Health.

Further references

Muir Gray J. A. (2004) *The Resourceful Patient*. Kent: Kent County Council and the Smith Institute.

Department of Education and Skills (2003) *Every Child Matters*. London: DES.

Department of Education and Skills (2004) *The Next Steps*. London: DES.

Department of Health (2002) *Delivering the NHS Plan: Next steps on Investment, next steps on reform*. London: DoH.

Department of Health (1998) *Modernising Social Services: Promoting Independence, Improving Protection, Raising Standards*. London: DoH.

Department of Health (1997) *The New NHS: Modern, dependable*. London: DoH.

Department of Health (2004) *The NHS Improvement Plan: Putting people at the heart of public services*. London: DoH.

Department of Health (2000) *The NHS Plan: A plan for investment, a plan for reform*. London: DoH.

Wanless D. (2002) *Securing our Future Health: Taking a long term view*. London: HM Treasury.

Wanless D. (2004) *Securing good health for the whole population: Final Report*. London: HM Treasury.